GET
TAROT!

Andrews McMeel Publishing
a division of Andrews McMeel Universal
1130 Walnut Street, Kansas City, Missouri 64106

www.andrewsmcmeel.com

First published in 2023 by White Star s.r.l.

Vivida

Vivida® is a trademark property of White Star s.r.l.
www.vividabooks.com
©2023 White Star s.r.l.
Piazzale Luigi Cadorna, 6
20123 Milan, Italy
www.whitestar.it

23 24 25 26 27 SDB 10 9 8 7 6 5 4 3 2 1

ISBN: 978-1-5248-8126-9

Editor: Katie Gould
Designer: Tiffany Meairs
Production Editor: Julie Railsback
Production Manager: Tamara Haus

ATTENTION: SCHOOLS AND BUSINESSES
Andrews McMeel books are available at quantity discounts with
bulk purchase for educational, business, or sales promotional use.
For information, please e-mail the Andrews McMeel Publishing
Special Sales Department: sales@amuniversal.com.

EDITED BY
FRANCESCA MATTEONI

GET TAROT!

A Perfect Guidebook
to Practice
Tarot Reading

Andrews McMeel
PUBLISHING®

TABLE OF CONTENTS

HOW TO USE THIS BOOK

The 78 cards in a tarot deck are extraordinary tools for exploring the self, destiny, and inner and collective dimensions. You can use them to meditate and sharpen your outlook on a given situation. This book is designed as a journal of practices for understanding the meanings of the cards. You can write down your impressions, answer questions, add ideas, and continue to work on your notebook, returning to the exercises and modifying your answers over time.

The beauty of intuitive work with tarot cards is that they are sensitive to the moment and the experience. Each time, you can immerse yourself in the figures, bringing in what is happening outside, seeking out a way to your dreams.

Without you, the images do not speak.

They need to be looked at actively to reveal themselves.

Think of them as a map. Each time they will show you a different destination, pleasantly surprise you, or tell you something you couldn't focus on.

You can open and consult the book at your leisure, with no obligation to complete each section. You may find exercises that you do not know how to answer immediately. If you have questions, just write them down on the pages for later reference.

You will also find many quotes. Use them as additional clues, puzzles that only you can solve and utilize later on in life.

Tarot cards are full of possibilities and contingencies, so don't worry if the definitions you find are different from the more classic ones. Each new way of looking at them adds a word or detail.

AND NOW, AS WITH ALL BEAUTIFUL STORIES,
LET'S START THE JOURNEY!

CHAPTER 1

Major Arcana

THE FOOL

"Not all those who wander are lost."

J.R.R. TOLKIEN

The Fool has no number. He can be found at any season of life. Every adventure is born from his imagination and ability to believe in the impossible. There are no age limits to journeying. It starts many times, mends broken roads, and follows the inspiration of a moment or a lifetime.

REMEMBER:

Every journey begins by getting lost.

Innocence leads to beauty.

Hold on to wonder.

Believe in the invisible.

In the presence of chaos, seek the ground underfoot.

MATCHES AND KINDRED SPIRITS:

- **Little Red Riding Hood** leaving the path, going to meet her destiny. The wolf is not always an adversary.

- **Alice** falling down a hole chasing the White Rabbit in *Alice in Wonderland* by Lewis Carroll. She travels through illusions, visions, and paradoxes.

- **The Fool** in *King Lear*, the Shakespearean court jester who intuitively identifies the nature of events and people without incurring punishment.

- **The Fairy Fool** of the Irish tradition, the Amadan-na-Breena recounted by W.B. Yeats in *The Celtic Twilight*, who is powerful and unpredictable.

- **The child** in Hans Christian Andersen's fairy tale *The Emperor's New Clothes*, who exclaims "The king is naked!" and tells the truth.

THE FOOL IN MUSIC:

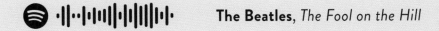

The Beatles, *The Fool on the Hill*

SHARE A TIME WHEN YOU LOST YOUR WAY, BY CHOICE OR DESTINY, AND HOW IT HAPPENED

CREATE A LIST OF THINGS
YOU BELIEVED IN AS A CHILD . . .

....

....

....

....

....

....

AND THOSE YOU STILL BELIEVE IN

....

....

....

....

....

....

THE MAGICIAN

"*I intend to be, and I mean it,
the Prince of Thieves.*"

HOMERIC HYMN TO HERMES

The Magician has the power of self-determination in the presence of himself and others. He focuses on his goal and employs all his tools to achieve it . . . no matter the cost. He chronicles, creates, conjures, demonstrates, and sometimes steals, cheats, and tricks. Power, after all, is the most enduring of illusions.

THE MAGICIAN

REMEMBER:

Determination pushes talent to reality.

Know your tools.

Magic is the illusion that sustains this world.

There are many versions of one story
that vary according to place, time, and narrator.

Creating and destroying at will
is not always the best choice.

MATCHES AND KINDRED SPIRITS:

+ **Hermes**, messenger of the gods in Greek mythology, protector of travelers, god of thieves and merchants, guardian of borders.

+ **Prospero**, exiled duke and magician in William Shakespeare's play *The Tempest*, whose magic controls, conjures, and ultimately liberates.

+ **Circe**, enchantress and minor goddess in Homer's *Odyssey*, turns men into lovers and beasts at her will.

+ **The little girl Pippi Longstocking**, invented by Astrid Lindgren: autonomous, nonconformist, and a great liar.

+ **The trickster** of Native American lore, sometimes human, sometimes animal, who solves the tribe's problems by bursting in with his mayhem and eccentricities.

THE MAGICIAN IN MUSIC:

   **Steeleye Span**, *Two Magicians*

WRITE YOUR BIOGRAPHY IN THREE LINES. THEN WRITE YOUR MADE-UP BIOGRAPHY IN THREE MORE LINES. COMPARE THEM

SET THREE OBJECTIVES FOR YOURSELF, BEGINNING EACH SENTENCE WITH "I WANT." AFTERWARD, WRITE HOW YOU MIGHT ACHIEVE THEM

....
....
....
....
....
....
....
....
....
....
....

THE HIGH PRIESTESS

*"This is my letter to the World that never wrote to me—
the simple news that nature told—with tender Majesty."*

EMILY DICKINSON

The High Priestess silently receives messages from the world around her and draws her deep wisdom from intuition, which creates an inner space of immersion and welcome in the most hidden part of ourselves. The High Priestess dwells among the ancestors and speaks their language. She sees the world with her eyes closed, with the foresight of her soul.

REMEMBER:

Sometimes it is necessary to be still and listen.

The community in which we dwell is composed of the living and the dead, bodies and spirits.

Those who accept the power of the past prepare for the future. It is not possible to understand everything; so rely on water, where the languages of the world mingle, always flowing from and toward life.

You can remain invisible as long as necessary, without abandoning contact with the world.

MATCHES AND KINDRED SPIRITS:

- **The Cumaean Sibyl** in her cave, writing the future on leaves and showing the path to reunite with loved ones in Book Six of Virgil's *Aeneid*.

- **Pythia**, the oracle of Greek tradition, who can speak in the tongue of great serpents in an ecstatic trance.

- **The Elder-Tree Mother**, lady of remembrance, in Hans Christian Andersen's fairy tale of the same name.

- **Lady Galadriel,** who observes fate in the water in J.R.R. Tolkien's *The Lord of the Rings* series.

- **Emily Dickinson**, who lived all possible lives behind a window.

THE HIGH PRIESTESS IN MUSIC:

Björk, *Pagan Poetry*

OBSERVE THE LANDSCAPE AROUND YOU IN ALL ITS ELEMENTS. WRITE DOWN HOW YOU FEEL ABOUT EACH LIFE YOU OBSERVE

THINK ABOUT YOUR DEAD LOVED ONES AND CHOOSE ONE. WRITE WHAT THEY PASSED ON TO YOU AND WHAT THEY STILL TEACH YOU

THE EMPRESS

NAVAJO NIGHT CHANT

In the woods, in the rubble, in a place of passing, the Empress nurtures what is around her with her imagination. She creates and opens pathways, overthrows and regenerates tradition, and labors to heal the wounds of the cosmos because they belong to her. She inhabits strong feelings that either exalt or destroy her. Her intelligence seeks shelter in the world.

REMEMBER:

It is necessary to concentrate to realize one dream at a time.

You can live among others because they are part of you.

The power to heal is greater than any reckoning.

Every wound is a rift where a forest is born.

To live with love is to let go.

MATCHES AND KINDRED SPIRITS:

+ **The little girl Wendy** in J.M. Barrie's *The Adventures of Peter Pan* as she learns the value of growing up.

+ **The Celtic witch Ceridwen**, mistress of poetic inspiration.

+ **The Great Mother** of prehistoric cultures and new spiritualities.

+ **Red-headed Anne**, the orphan protagonist of *Anne of Green Gables* by L.M. Montgomery, who cares for the little ones and has a thirst for learning.

+ **Lyra Belacqua** or **Lyra Silvertongue**, the passionate and courageous child protagonist of Philip Pullman's *His Dark Materials* trilogy, who sets out to save a friend.

THE EMPRESS IN MUSIC:

 **Leonard Cohen,** *Suzanne*

WHO OR WHAT DO YOU CARE FOR?
MAKE A LIST AND WRITE A BRIEF DESCRIPTION FOR EACH ITEM

DESCRIBE HOW YOU WOULD LIKE OTHERS TO CARE FOR YOU

....

....

....

....

....

....

....

....

....

....

....

....

✦ THE EMPEROR ✦

"Love and do what you wish."
St. Augustine

The Emperor holds the power of boundaries. He knows the boundaries, observes them, and returns them to us so that our will might be more determined and clear. The Emperor does not oppress or command, but chooses who and what to love, shaping ideas. In him is the experience of the difference between authority and authoritativeness. His eyes do not judge, but rather offer support.

IV

THE EMPEROR

REMEMBER:

✦☾

Power comes through direct experience
of the world and of others.

To know the end of things is to set them free.

To lay down the sword takes more will than to draw it.

To return reality to others is the purpose of control.

To control oneself requires great vulnerability.

MATCHES AND KINDRED SPIRITS:

- **Aragorn in Middle-earth**, reluctant king who learns to return after exile, in J.R.R. Tolkien's *The Lord of the Rings* books.

- **The Fisher King in Welsh mythology**, whose health is linked to that of the land and who humbly asks others to heal him.

- **The rabbit Hazel** in Richard Adams's *Watership Down*, leading her community to a new home through understanding and trust.

- **Young David**, second king of Israel, using intelligence to defeat brute force in the books of the *Bible*.

- **Morgana**, a fairy and King Arthur's sister, who accepts that her world recedes so she might stay, in Marion Zimmer Bradley's novel *The Mists of Avalon*.

THE EMPEROR IN MUSIC:

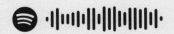 **David Bowie**, *The Man Who Sold the World*

WRITE A LIST OF THINGS YOU HAVE POWER OVER AND EXPLAIN HOW YOU EXERCISE IT

....

....

....

....

....

....

....

....

....

....

....

....

WRITE A LIST OF MOMENTS WHEN YOU FELT THE OPPRESSION OF POWER AND THE DESIRE TO REBEL TO REDEFINE YOUR BOUNDARIES

THE HIEROPHANT

"Aim at heaven and you will get earth thrown in.
Aim at earth and you get neither."

C.S. LEWIS

The Hierophant is the master who guards tradition. He shows the paths that have been traveled and can be traveled, inviting the quest for independence. The Hierophant represents education and crisis. When he appears, you must learn that no knowledge is exhaustive. His greatest teaching allows one to rise above the known, opening up the gates to the future.

V

THE HIEROPHANT

REMEMBER:

Every tradition is constantly being reinvented.

To learn is to stand in crisis.

A good teacher wants to be surpassed by their students.

Whoever educates blesses and guides the world.

Studying is the first step to dreaming up growth.

MATCHES AND KINDRED SPIRITS:

—✦— **The lion Aslan** in *The Chronicles of Narnia* by C.S. Lewis,
whose sacred power awakens the Enchanted Land.
As a good spiritual teacher, he allows the child protagonists
to have their own experiences of life.

—✦— **Virgil** in Dante's *Divine Comedy*, guide and teacher
who knows when to be silent and when to intervene.

—✦— **Saraswati**, Hindu goddess from whom writing, the arts,
and everything that expresses knowledge and tradition come.

—✦— **The cat** who, despite being terrified of heights,
helps the little seagull take flight in Luis Sepúlveda's novel
The Story of a Seagull and the Cat Who Taught Her to Fly.

THE HIEROPHANT IN MUSIC:

Pink Floyd, *Another Brick in the Wall*

WRITE A LIST OF THINGS YOU HAVE LEARNED, AND DESCRIBE WHO TAUGHT THEM TO YOU

DESCRIBE A TIME OF CRISIS WITH SOCIETY AND ITS USES. MAKE A LIST OF THINGS YOU WOULD LIKE TO CHANGE

✦ LOVERS ✦

"Love set you going
Like a fat gold watch."
SYLVIA PLATH

We stand in the presence of the love, beauty, and desire that motivate our actions. The Lovers embody the essence of the choice we are called to make when we meet another on our path. In tarot decks, lovers entrust each other with dedication, agreeing to give up something of themselves to enter the moment of shared life.

REMEMBER:

To love is to rely on the other while giving him or her shelter.

You can choose your fellow travelers.

No matter how many mistakes you make in life, what counts above all else is to have loved.

You can learn to find the best part of yourself in another.

Look for those who see your worth.

MATCHES AND KINDRED SPIRITS:

✦ **Jane Eyre and Mr. Rochester**, who find each other in difficulties and finally experience love in Charlotte Brontë's novel *Jane Eyre*.

✦ **Eros and Psyche**, symbols in Greek mythology of knowing another through loss.

✦ **Scarlett O'Hara**, protagonist of Margaret Mitchell's novel *Gone with the Wind*, in her long lesson about love: for the earth, for herself, for a companion.

✦ **The fairies** who deceive, seduce, and play with lovers in William Shakespeare's *A Midsummer Night's Dream*.

✦ **The dog Buck** in Jack London's *The Call of the Wild*, who experiences love for humans and later chooses his wild nature.

LOVERS IN MUSIC:

 **Nick Cave**, *The Ship Song*

WRITE A LIST OF THE THINGS AND PEOPLE YOU LOVE AND HAVE LOVED, AND ASSOCIATE THEM WITH A STATE OF MIND

WRITE WHEN LOVE BECOMES AN OBSESSION FOR YOU AND HOW YOU GOT OUT OF IT OR MIGHT GET OUT OF IT

....

....

....

....

....

....

....

....

....

....

....

✦ The Chariot ✦

"Perform all actions by abandoning attachment to the fruits of actions, being indifferent to success and failure."

Bhagavad Gita, 2, 48

To ride the Chariot is to take control of one's desires in order to take the path of destiny. The Chariot represents ambition, the ability to aim directly for a goal, working confidently to achieve it. In the Arcana, however, it is also necessary to remember that the journey is often more important than the destination and may hold surprises.

REMEMBER:

✦☾

Willpower drives and sustains talent.

Every goal achieved is a new beginning.

The best journey is one that leaves no one behind.

Persevering in the quest can lead down unexpected and happy paths.

As you advance on the path, it is good to observe the details as well.

MATCHES AND KINDRED SPIRITS:

-+- **The archer Arjuna**, advised by the god Krishna, in the guise of his chariot driver, who on the battlefield must decide whether to act or retreat from combat, in the Hindu sacred text *Bhagavad Gita*.

-+- **The carriage** that leads Cinderella to her destiny in the famous fairy tale.

-+- **Fùcur**, the Dragon of Fortune ridden by Atreiu in search of the savior of the land of Fantasia in Michael Ende's *The Neverending Story*.

-+- **Phileas Fogg**, who attempts to circumnavigate the world in eighty days on a bet (and succeeds), in Jules Verne's novel *Around the World in Eighty Days*.

-+- **The Wild Hunt** in the autumn skies of Europe, by which spirits and the dead are reunited with the living according to Celtic and Germanic tradition.

THE CHARIOT IN MUSIC:

 **The Doors**, *Riders On the Storm*

THINK OF AN ACCOMPLISHED GOAL IN YOUR LIFE. WRITE DOWN HOW YOU ACHIEVED IT, WHO HELPED YOU, WHAT YOU WOULD CHANGE, AND WHAT HAPPENED NEXT

....

....

....

....

....

....

....

....

....

....

....

....

VISUALIZE YOUR DEEPEST WISHES.
MAKE A LIST OF THEM THAT BEGINS WITH
"I STRIVE FOR"

✦ STRENGTH ✦

*"Only he who has measured the dominion of force, and knows
how not to respect it, is capable of love and justice."*

SIMONE WEIL

This card asks us: What is true strength? It asks us to look at the soul, which
has a wild and untamed form, speaking to it with kindness. It asks us to learn
to surrender and accept, not to retreat from the shocks and wounds, to make
them our armor. Strength is exposed and vulnerable. In pain, it takes a deep
breath and then smiles.

REMEMBER:

✦☾

It takes as much strength to hold on
as it does to know when to give up.

Those who are strong never interrupt
the dialogue with fragility.

You can choose to live with your dark sides instead
of stubbornly trying to overcome them without
understanding them.

Looking for wildness in each day is an act of hope.

Sometimes, courage falls silent and observes.

MATCHES AND KINDRED SPIRITS:

—+— **Joan of Arc**, armed only with her faith in the dull march of war.

—+— The courage and love of books described by **Maya Angelou** in her autobiographical novel, *I Know Why the Caged Bird Sings*, against the traumas of racial violence.

—+— **Mowgli**, the child adopted by wolves in Rudyard Kipling's *The Jungle Book*, whose strength is his knowledge of all animal languages.

—+— **Gerda**, who in Hans Christian Andersen's fairy tale *The Snow Queen* braves the frost to bring her friend Kai home.

—+— **Ruthie Fear**, in Maxim Loskutoff's novel of the same name, able to accept defeat, pain, and fate by choosing her imperfect human community.

STRENGTH IN MUSIC:

   **Pixies**, *Caribou*

MAKE TWO LISTS FOR STRENGTH: IN THE FIRST, LIST EVERYTHING YOU CONSIDER ABUSE OR VIOLENCE; IN THE SECOND, PUT WHAT YOU RECOGNIZE AS COURAGE OR RESISTANCE

STRENGTH IS ALSO A CARD FOR CONTACT
WITH ANIMALS. IMAGINE THE ANIMAL THAT INHABITS
YOU ACCORDING TO YOUR FEELINGS, AND DESCRIBE IT.
TRY TO IDENTIFY AN ANIMAL FOR RAGE,
LOVE, FEAR, AND SO ON

....

....

....

....

....

....

....

....

....

✦ THE HERMIT ✦

"My sorrow—I could not awaken
My heart to joy at the same tone—
And all I lov'd—I lov'd alone—"

EDGAR ALLAN POE

On the mountain path, the Hermit lights his lamp, which shines with his purpose and dreams. He advances slowly, occasionally stopping to contemplate the landscape below or to converse with the stars. His solitude is full of words and revelations. The Hermit asks to devote himself to the search for truth and personal essence.

IX

THE HERMIT

REMEMBER:

☾

All light comes out of the cracks in the shadow, like the soul emerging from a cloak.

You can marvel at the lessons everything has to offer.

No loneliness is sad if the gaze is open and the heart converses with the living.

When you don't know how to solve a situation, stop, meditate, and observe.

Be your own companion.

MATCHES AND KINDRED SPIRITS:

- ┼ The slowness of **Treebeard of Ent**, the tree herders in *Middle-earth* invented by J.R.R. Tolkien. His wisdom is ancient and countercultural.

- ┼ **The Biblical necromancer** of the city of Endor, exiled by the king who communicates with the spirits of the dead.

- ┼ **Henry David Thoreau** when he decided to live in a cabin in Walden Wood for two years.

- ┼ **Han Shan**, Chinese poet and hermit with a birchbark hat, who lived and wrote on the Cold Mountain.

THE HERMIT IN MUSIC:

 **Fleet Foxes**, *Tiger Mountain Peasant Song*

IMAGINE OR REMEMBER A SECRET PLACE FROM YOUR CHILDHOOD. TAKE REFUGE THERE WITH YOUR MIND, AND DESCRIBE IT

MAKE TWO LISTS FOR SOLITUDE. IN THE FIRST, LIST THE NEGATIVE ASPECTS; IN THE SECOND, THE POSITIVE ONES

THE WHEEL OF FORTUNE

"Learn only to seize fortune."
JOHANN WOLFGANG VON GOETHE

We are all born on the Wheel of Fortune, which never stops turning, leading us to see reality from different angles: some uncomfortable, some privileged, none unchanging. How does one deal with fate? Anticipating its moves, trying to evade it? The Wheel brings change, something new. It invites us to know that not everything can be controlled.

THE WHEEL OF FORTUNE

REMEMBER:

Every ending inevitably merges into a beginning.

What is planned can be disrupted by an unpredictable fact.

Maintain a conversation with your good fortune, with adversity, with the unknown.

You can find opportunity even in the adverse side of fate.

Your destiny adapts and fluctuates with that of the world.

MATCHES AND KINDRED SPIRITS:

- **The three goddesses of fate** in Greco-Roman tradition, intent on spinning, measuring, and cutting the thread of destiny.

- The unequal struggle between the **Malavoglia** family and their fate as fishermen, ruled by the sea, in Giovanni Verga's novel of the same name.

- **The orphan Pip**, protagonist of Charles Dickens's *Great Expectations*, who must protect the value of friendship and love in the face of surprising fate.

THE WHEEL OF FORTUNE IN MUSIC:

   **Joni Mitchell,** *The Circle Game*

WRITE ABOUT A TIME WHEN LIFE HAS SURPRISED YOU, BOTH POSITIVELY AND NEGATIVELY. DESCRIBE HOW IT CHANGED YOU

....

....

....

....

....

....

....

....

....

....

....

ADDRESS A PRAYER TO THE WHEEL, IMAGINING YOURSELF ON TOP OF IT WHILE IT IS IN MOTION

✦ JUSTICE ✦

> *"Do not suppose that I have come to bring peace to the earth.*
> *I did not come to bring peace, but a sword."*
>
> ### GOSPEL OF MATTHEW 10:34-36

Justice rights wrongs and redistributes merit far beyond the courtrooms. It is the cosmic law that governs us and resonates deep within ourselves. Every day, Justice rephrases the question: What is right? Why do we suffer? Where will we find compensation for our struggles? The answer shines somewhere on the edge of the sword.

REMEMBER:

✦☽

What seems unjust in our history
is diluted in the living of the universe.

Keep a light heart, so that even a storm
may lift it without damage.

Things work out with or without our help,
but all things cooperate for good.

Justice is a nonaggressive pact with the soul
of the world.

Loyalty and humility are the sisters of Justice.

MATCHES AND KINDRED SPIRITS:

- **Atticus Finch**, father of Scout, the little girl protagonist in Harper Lee's novel *To Kill a Mockingbird*, who explains to his children why sparrows should not be shot, their mocking cry their only defense.

- **Sedna**, Mother of the Sea Animals of Inuit tradition, exiled and killed by her community in human form, who becomes a dispenser of food or famine from the depths of the sea.

- **Mabel**, the goshawk in Helen Macdonald's novel *H is for Hawk*, who, amidst the tragedy of a sudden loss, helps the woman recognize the fierce dignity of what continues to exist.

- The forgiveness and spiritual justice of **Alexei Karamazov** in Fyodor Dostoevsky's novel *The Brothers Karamazov* act as the paths to wisdom and innocence.

- **God**, revealing to Job the greatness of the cosmos compared to the pain of an individual human.

JUSTICE IN MUSIC:

Bob Dylan, *Knockin' On Heaven's Door*

WHEN DO YOU FIND YOURSELF FEELING THAT SOMETHING IS UNFAIR? AND WHEN DO YOU FEEL THAT'S OKAY? MAKE A LIST

....

....

....

....

....

....

....

....

....

....

....

WRITE AN IMAGINARY CONTRACT WITH YOUR SOUL, ESTABLISHING WHAT VALUES SHOULD BE RESPECTED AND WHAT YOU WANT TO ACHIEVE TOGETHER

✦ THE HANGED MAN ✦

"I rest not from my great task!
To open the Eternal Worlds, to open the immortal Eyes
Of Man inwards into the Worlds of Thought: into Eternity
Ever expanding in the Bosom of God, the Human Imagination."
WILLIAM BLAKE

The Hanged Man turns upside down to get a different view of reality. He needs to invert his perspective, to interrupt his daily journey and embark on a spiritual one, wandering through other worlds while the body is still in the present. In the Hanged Man card, we experience the power of sacrificial love, of conscious surrender of self in the name of higher knowledge.

XII

THE HANGED MAN

REMEMBER:

Clarity is a light that can flow from within.

Do not underestimate the wait; in the meantime, know your potential.

You can listen to the voice that says, "Dive in, touch the bottom, see what blooms down there."

When things are incomprehensible, it is possible to reverse our perspective and reflect.

No sacrifice should lead to the annihilation of the self.

MATCHES AND KINDRED SPIRITS:

- **Odin**, father of the gods in Scandinavian mythology, hanging from the cosmic tree to let the runes of knowledge flow from his head.

- **The goddess Luonnotar** of the Finnish epic poem "Kalevala," fertilized by wind and waves, who carried the weight of her pregnancy for seven hundred years, creating the world.

- **The spider Charlotte**, suspended from her thread, who invisibly helps piglet Wilbur survive, in the book *Charlotte's Web* by E.B. White.

- **The Phoenician sailor Fleba**, drowned and ready to rise again in the poem *The Waste Land* by T.S. Eliot.

- **The waiting of the Selkie**, a creature of Celtic tradition who, deprived of her seal skin, lives for years as a devoted wife and mother until she can return to the ocean.

THE HANGED MAN IN MUSIC:

   Tori Amos, *Crucify*

TRY LOOKING AT YOURSELF THROUGH THE EYES OF OTHERS. DESCRIBE YOURSELF BY ADOPTING THE PERSPECTIVE OF SOMEONE CLOSE TO YOU

WRITE DOWN WHEN AND HOW YOU CAN BE OF HELP WHILE STANDING IN THE SHADOWS

✦ DEATH ✦

"Death, o little one, is not to sleep, but to rise,
Not to sleep, but to return."

MARINA CVETAEVA

Death is traditionally the nameless Arcana card, the mystery that makes our living unique and precious. Before Death, we do not stand before an unforgiving end, but rather enter a transformative process to leave behind the skin that no longer serves us. In Death, we prepare ourselves to don the robe of the future.

REMEMBER:

☾

We die many times in a single existence.

Death marks the end of a cycle.
We must go through it with serenity.

Lingering on something completed brings
no long-term benefits, only illusions.

Becoming aware of dying means reactivating personal
and collective memory.
Everything is transformation: the caterpillar, chrysalis,
and butterfly exist in you at different times.

MATCHES AND KINDRED SPIRITS:

+ **Philemon and Baucis**, earthly spouses of Greek mythology who were transformed by Zeus after their death into an oak tree and a linden tree with intertwined trunks.

+ The fall into the abyss of the sorcerer **Gandalf the Grey** and his return as Gandalf the White in Tolkien's Middle-earth.

+ **Siddhartha Gautauma,** reaching the Nirvana and becoming Buddha in Indian tradition.

+ **Gilgamesh**, the hero of the Babylonian epic who searches for and loses the plant of immortality, accepting his human destiny.

DEATH IN MUSIC:

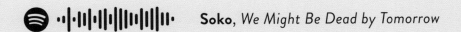

Soko, *We Might Be Dead by Tomorrow*

THINK ABOUT THE IMPORTANT PASSAGES IN YOUR LIFE AND WRITE THEM DOWN. WRITE WHAT YOU HAVE LOST AND WHAT YOU HAVE FOUND

....

....

....

....

....

....

....

....

....

....

....

THINK ABOUT THE VERB "TO DIE" AND FIND OTHER VERBS, POSITIVE OR NEGATIVE, THAT CAN EXPRESS ITS VARIOUS MEANINGS

✦ TEMPERANCE ✦

"Everything is full and upset,
everything, dark, triumphs and prostrates."
ANDREA ZANZOTTO

Temperance is an angel who mixes the waters of two different jugs: good and evil, desires and needs, ourselves and others. In doing so, she becomes the guardian of life and its changes. She doesn't so much reveal a moderate use of our energy as she shares the constant adjustment of our way of feeling to that of the world.

REMEMBER:

Temperance alchemically unites opposites;
it dispenses with nothing.

Everything good is always accompanied
by equally great darkness: know them both.

The harmonious balance of parts is the effort
to grow among others.

You can find balance by going through excess and difficulty.

In adversity and beauty, everything is spoken
and held anyway.

MATCHES AND KINDRED SPIRITS:

+ **Beatrice** when she encounters Dante in the Earthly Paradise: severity and forgiveness mutually exist in her.

+ **The mysterious angel Skellig**, protagonist of David Almond's novel of the same name, who feeds on spiders and lives in a garage but who helps save the life of a newborn girl, sister of the child protagonist.

+ **Soothsayer Balaam's donkey**, the only creature to see the angel of the Lord on the way to the land of Moab in a biblical episode.

TEMPERANCE IN MUSIC:

Led Zeppelin, *Stairway to Heaven*

WHICH OF YOUR ASPECTS CAN AND SHOULD YOU MAKE MORE HARMONIC? MAKE A LIST

....

....

....

....

....

....

....

....

....

....

....

THINK OF TIMES WHEN
YOU HAVE FELT PROTECTION IN YOUR LIFE.
DESCRIBE THEM

....

....

....

....

....

....

....

....

....

....

....

✦ THE DEVIL ✦

*"If I didn't believe in life, if I lost faith in the woman I love,
lost faith in the order of things, were convinced in fact that everything
is a disorderly, damnable, and perhaps devil-ridden chaos,
if I were struck by every horror of man's disillusionment—
still I should want to live."*

FYODOR DOSTOEVSKY

The Devil raises his flashlight and illuminates the paths that open beyond his body. To travel them, one must face him, knowing the value of light. The Devil represents instinctual power, passion, the ability to go against the tide, but also uncontrolled surrender to the life of our senses. Breaking free from our chains is an act of will.

REMEMBER:

We forge in ourselves the most insidious chains.

You need not fear the dark but, as you walk,
always look for a bright spot.

The Devil divides, deceives, and reveals
for those who dare not look away.

Lift your spirit from material happiness
to more lasting joy, but do not forget that from the body
we depart and to it we return.

Whatever happens, don't devalue
or repress your passion: create boundaries for it.

MATCHES AND KINDRED SPIRITS:

+ **Paolo and Francesca** in Dante's *Inferno* and all the unhappy lovers who lived and died by their passion.

+ **The devil** in the fairy tale *The Handless Maiden* by the Grimm Brothers, unable to take possession of herself or her soul.

+ **The god Pan** in Greek mythology, who stirs up wild nature and sexuality in opposition to conformity.

+ **Heathcliff**, a tormented man in Emily Brontë's novel *Wuthering Heights*, whose spirit is reflected on the moors, who finds peace only in the grave, beside the woman he longed for above all else.

+ **The devil Woland** in *The Master and Margarita*, who came to Moscow as a professor, an expert in magic, bringing chaos, subversion, and vitality.

THE DEVIL IN MUSIC:

The Rolling Stones, *Sympathy for the Devil*

THINK ABOUT WHEN YOU FEEL TRAPPED, AND DESCRIBE THE SITUATION. DOES IT HAPPEN TO YOU OFTEN? IS IT A SITUATION THAT REPEATS ITSELF? HOW CAN YOU GET OUT OF IT?

DESCRIBE ALL YOUR FEARS AND IMAGINE HOW TO LIVE NEXT TO THEM, WITHOUT LETTING THEM OVERWHELM YOU

✦ THE TOWER ✦

> *"Come after me, and let the people talk;*
> *Stand like a steadfast tower, that never wags*
> *Its top for all the blowing of the winds;*
>
> *For evermore the man in whom is springing*
> *Thought upon thought, removes from him the mark,*
> *Because the force of one the other weakens."*
>
> ### DANTE ALIGHIERI

The Tower is broken by lightning, like an omen of doom: collapse, end, devastation. Every dream crumbles. Yet the light that bursts from the sky is also revelatory. It removes all illusion and annihilates arrogance. Reduced to rubble, the walls of the Tower give way to the landscape and the horizon, and consciousness, in trauma, awakens.

XVI

THE TOWER

REMEMBER:

☽

You can stand in the confusion, collapse, and end of a world without disappearing.

Human ambition cannot do without the world, which dictates its limits and scale.

The truth exists even in destruction; recover what you care about and look for another way.

Changes can be drastic. Accept them. Start over.

Sometimes fleeing and deserting is better than staying and struggling.

MATCHES AND KINDRED SPIRITS:

—|— **The ancient Tower** full of slits where poet W.B. Yeats spent much of his elderly life, taking inspiration for his greatest poem.

—|— **Rapunzel** from the classic fairy tale, lost until freed outside the tower.

—|— **The two Towers** symbolize power in J.R.R. Tolkien's Middle-earth.

—|— **Father and son** in Cormac McCarthy's novel *The Road*, venturing out together on a devastated planet.

THE TOWER IN MUSIC:

 **The Cure**, *Disintegration*

WRITE ABOUT A TIME WHEN A MAJOR CHANGE OCCURRED IN YOUR LIFE. WHAT TRIGGERED IT? WHAT DID YOU LEARN? HOW DID YOU BEGIN AGAIN?

THE TOWER COLLAPSED. DESCRIBE
EVERYTHING YOU SEE BEFORE YOU

....

....

....

....

....

....

....

....

....

....

....

....

....

✦ THE STAR ✦

*"I see the stars flame, high
in the purest blue,
mirrored far off by the sea:
the universe glittering with sparks
that wheel through the tranquil void."*

GIACOMO LEOPARDI

By the river, in the night, one encounters a meek creature who pours water on a stone or simply exposes itself, nude. She is the Star who came down to Earth as the daughter of all humans. She comforts us in suffering, creeps gently into the soul, making it shine. Every dream, in her, is worthy and true.

XVII

THE STAR

REMEMBER:

✦☽

You exist in the world to dream to the skies,
which is your home just like the Earth.

The Star comes down unarmed.
Disarm yourself before her.

You can build hope in the present
by turning desires into seeds.

The Star speaks to the downtrodden and to the fragile part
of us, so that it may rise and heal us.

When all is lost, shine.

MATCHES AND KINDRED SPIRITS:

+ **The last gift** of Pandora's open box, containing all the evils of the world in Greek mythology, was hope.

+ **The slow and stubborn dialogue of trees with existence** at this time of crisis in the book *The Overstory* by Richard Powers.

+ **The fairy-star** fallen to Earth in Neil Gaiman's novel *Stardust*, rescued by the love of a human being.

THE STAR IN MUSIC:

   **Portishead**, *Wandering Star*

WHERE HAVE YOU PLACED YOUR HOPE? MAKE A LIST, WRITING ON INSTINCT

WHAT DOES IT MEAN TO HEAL FROM WOUNDS? GIVE SOME PERSONAL EXAMPLES

✦ THE MOON ✦

> *"On the grey rock of Cashel the mind's eye*
> *Has called up the cold spirits that are born*
> *When the old moon is vanished from the sky*
> *And the new still hides her horn."*
>
> **WILLIAM BUTLER YEATS**

The Moon watches over the shadowy sides of ourselves: the dream universe, the unconscious, the perception of the future, but also our anxieties, illusions, and repressed emotions. The animal stretches its snout toward her and howls or sings, depending on how willing we are to accompany it. The Moon invites us to face deception, calling it out with her white light.

XVIII

THE MOON

REMEMBER:

☽

There is a map in your nocturnal dreams. Decipher it. Rely on instinct when vision is blurred.

Feed your approach to existence, remembering that nothing is ever as it seems and everything dies and returns again and again.

Take care of your instability; occasionally cradle your Moon.

On a sea voyage, remember the vastness hidden below.

MATCHES AND KINDRED SPIRITS:

✧ **The Moon addressed by the shepherd** in the poem *Night Song of a Wandering Shepherd in Asia* by Giacomo Leopardi.

✧ **The Moon buried in the swamp by evil spirits** and freed by a man so that she might return to heaven more splendid, told in an English fairy tale of the same name.

✧ **Astolfo traveling to the moon** to recover the lost wits of the hero Orlando, in Ludovico Ariosto's chivalric poem "Orlando Furioso."

✧ **Hecate**, queen of demons and ghosts, guardian of borders and crossroads under the Moon in Greek mythology.

THE MOON IN MUSIC:

   **Nick Drake**, *Pink Moon*

LOOK AT THE MOON, AND WRITE DOWN HOW IT MAKES YOU FEEL IN ITS DIFFERENT PHASES (WAXING, FULL, WANING, NEW)

CREATE A LIST OF ILLUSIONS YOU MANAGED TO RECOGNIZE

....

....

....

....

....

....

....

....

....

....

....

The Sun

"As children do in the noon-sun."
ELIZABETH BARRETT BROWNING

The Sun is well-being, success, and shared happiness. Everything good is lit up by its light and makes us enjoy the present. The Sun shows how to be content with what we have around us, finally recognizing its value and uniqueness. In the glow of the daytime star, we too are revitalized, gaining self-confidence and expressing our creativity.

REMEMBER:

The Sun helps bring clarity inside and out.

You can rejoice every day over the little things. Wisdom is simple.

In the Sun all shadows recede.

Smile, dance, jump, return to childhood whenever you can.

Staying true to yourself also means forgetting yourself in the beauty of the day.

MATCHES AND KINDRED SPIRITS:

✦ **The setting sun** that Ponyboy, protagonist of Susan Eloise Hinton's novel *The Outsiders*, sees every night from his block. And it is the same one that sets over wealthy neighborhoods.

✦ **Tom Bombadil**, the Very Old and Fatherless, whose joyous life in Tolkein's Middle-earth carries on, immune to evil.

✦ **The Sun who sees all** but yields to the beauty of Juliet in the Shakespearean tragedy *Romeo and Juliet*.

THE SUN IN MUSIC:

The Velvet Underground, *Ride Into the Sun*

WHAT ARE THE DAILY THINGS THAT MAKE YOU HAPPY? CREATE A LIST

....

....

....

....

....

....

....

....

....

....

....

....

WHAT CAN YOU DO TO REJOICE WITH OTHERS? DESCRIBE ONE OR MORE SITUATIONS

....

....

....

....

....

....

....

....

....

....

....

....

✦ JUDGMENT ✦

"This soul within my heart is bigger than the earth, bigger than atmospheric space, bigger than the sky, greater than the worlds."

CHĀNDOGYA UPANISHAD

In Judgment, our vocation rises from the ground and speaks to us. It sings like a swallow, sounds like the wind in flutes. We are awakened. After much waiting and wandering, Judgment allows us to live and express our full potential. In the card, reality and dreams finally coincide, as it has always been, an inner voice repeats to us.

XX

JUDGMENT

REMEMBER:

✦ ☽

You can begin to think of yourself in the future.

In Judgment, the future is already with you; it says, "Rise."

Everyone has a call to answer, which can be both frightening and joyful. When will you accept it?

In Judgment, criticize the past, appreciate it, make it a base from which to take flight.

It is never too late for it to be your time.

Time travels in a circle within the soul.

MATCHES AND KINDRED SPIRITS:

-+- **Nils Holgersson**, protagonist of Selma Lagerlöf's book
The Wonderful Journey of Nils Holgersson, who becomes a child
again after a year in the form of a leprechaun traveling
with wild geese and does not forget his animal companions.

-+- **Writer Janet Frame** in her autobiographical books: the long road
to knowing how to be happy with who you are, despite
all the suffering, estrangement, and misunderstanding of society.

-+- **The Ugly Duckling** from Hans Christian Andersen's fairy tale
of the same name, when he finally discovers that he
is the most beautiful of swans.

JUDGMENT IN MUSIC:

Patti Smith, *People Have the Power*

THINK ABOUT YOUR VOCATION. WHAT DO YOU KNOW HOW TO DO AND WHAT CAN YOU DO? WHAT HAVE YOU NOT YET TRIED? WHAT KIND OF FEAR IS STOPPING YOU AND HOW CAN YOU GET RID OF IT? WRITE ABOUT IT

Think of a difficult situation in your life. Describe it. Try to cultivate a vision. Imagine ways to exit

✦ THE WORLD ✦

> *"Whoever you are, no matter how lonely,*
> *the world offers itself to your imagination."*
> MARY OLIVER

The World is the end of the journey. When we reach it, we realize that we have always been there, that everything was already quiet and bright around us. But the most incredible of adventures is coming home, the rediscovery of what's known, understanding that nothing is taken for granted. In the World, we are home. We become its home.

XXI

THE WORLD

REMEMBER:

✦☽

Worlds are woven in invisible threads of love, hope, courage, and even fear.

Seek your belonging by opening the World to others.

Every day, something is broken so that it might live, and that is part of the beauty.

Do not reject disharmony; it is part of your uniqueness. Inhabit the intensity of surrender.

When the journey is over, scatter yourself across the landscape.

MATCHES AND KINDRED SPIRITS:

+ **The land of Fantasia**, threatened by the Nothing in Michael Ende's *The Neverending Story*, which only a human child can save.

+ **Neverland**, where Peter Pan and the Lost Boys dwell, in the tale of those who have returned.

+ **The many parallel worlds** separated by invisible boundaries in Philip Pullman's *His Dark Materials* trilogy.

+ **The sleep of the Hindu god Vishnu**, lying on the great serpent and adrift in the primeval waters, from which everything is generated like a dream.

+ **Little Dorothy** as she leaves the magical land of Oz and rediscovers familiar joy in the gray Kansas from which she came, in *The Wonderful Wizard of Oz* by L. Frank Baum.

THE WORLD IN MUSIC:

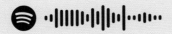 **Danit**, *Naturaleza*

DESCRIBE YOUR WORLDS; MAKE A LIST.
YOU CAN INCLUDE THE HOUSE WHERE YOU LIVED, THE PLACE WHERE YOU WORK, THE HOUSE WHERE YOU LIVE NOW, THE CITY, OR THE COUNTRY

DESCRIBE YOUR DREAM WORLD AND IMAGINE MAKING IT REAL

....

....

....

....

....

....

....

....

....

....

....

....

....

....

RELATIONSHIPS
BETWEEN MAJOR ARCANA CARDS

Below you will find some inspirational phrases that put together Major Arcana cards in pairs, trios, and quads, according to a common theme. Connections and correspondences can be made among all the Arcana cards.

- Every artist wears the clothes of the **Fool**, creates his universe in the **Magician**, and sees time reverse itself in the **Hanged Man**.

- Heal through the **Empress**'s embrace, the sisterhood between creatures in **Strength**, the hope of the **Stars**.

- Memory speaks to us through the insights and mysteries of the **High Priestess** and the cultural and family traditions of the **Hierophant**.

- Will makes its way in the **Emperor**, chooses in the **Lovers**, becomes resourceful in the **Chariot**, rises to wisdom in solitude in the **Hermit**.

- Forget who you are in the dream and the animals of the **Moon** before you shine in the **Sun**.

- Accept the alternate movement of the **Wheel** to know yourself in the **World**.

- Every existing thing has its course in **Justice**, is guarded by **Temperance**, finds its place in **Judgment**.

- Experience faces the **Devil** openly, can let go of the past in **Death**, restarts the path after the **Tower**.

REFLECT ON THE EXAMPLES GIVEN; IMAGINE AND MAKE YOUR OWN CONNECTIONS

CHAPTER 2

SUITS

✦ WANDS ✦

The Wands are associated with fire, spring, the driving energy of the spirit, the unpredictability of genius, and the light of those who rise up and endure in adverse times. Wands derive their vitality and destructiveness from fire; they embody its enthusiasm, passion, and ferocity. A purpose must be found each time, so as not to squander the great potential of the suit. And remember that others benefit or suffer from the consequences of our actions.

GUIDING WORDS

FLAIR

WILL

UNPREDICTABILITY

CHARISMA

NONCONFORMITY

ASSERTIVENESS

DEFENSE

CHOICE

VISION

PHYSICALITY

REMEMBER:

A wand can strike, defend, stand up,
be thrown into the air, and even flourish.

You can carry an impossible load of projects,
or you can choose what to keep and plant your own
little wand/tree.

Use fire to brighten, but burn it when it is dry
and no longer needed.

It warms those you love without smothering them.

When you use the power of the Wands
to destroy, take a bag of seeds with you
to start anew elsewhere.

Watch the future moving toward you,
do not be in a hurry.

Expose yourself to defend and not to attack.

SHARE IN A FEW LINES:

A SITUATION IN WHICH YOU ACTED UNPREDICTABLY AND WITH A POSITIVE OUTCOME.

....

....

....

A SITUATION IN WHICH YOU DEFENDED SOMETHING, SOMEONE, OR YOUR VALUES.

....

....

....

A SITUATION OF SHARED CELEBRATION AND JOY.

....

....

....

AN IMAGINATIVE GAME PLAYED IN CHILDHOOD.

....

....

....

✦ CUPS ✦

The Cups are associated with water, summer, emotionality, and the changeability of feelings, healing through knowledge of pain, deep and intimate dreams that animate our most important choices. Like water, the Cups welcome, refresh, heal; sometimes, however, within them we risk stagnation or being slowly overwhelmed by ourselves. The water of the Cups, on the other hand, should pour out freely: into our throats, onto the earth, and even out of our eyes through weeping.

GUIDING WORDS

FEELING

FRAGILITY

EMPATHY

WELCOME

REMEMBRANCE

COMPASSION

HARMONY

ADAPTABILITY

KINDNESS

VOLUBILITY

REMEMBER:

It is necessary to learn to swim in feelings,
as in the darkest and brightest ocean.

Do not keep the cup only for yourself;
pour it out elsewhere with care.

Drink from the cup of life, offer it,
fill it with memories and dreams.

Take it in.

In sorrow, do not feel victimized.
Let it pass without fear.

Always look beyond and beneath the surface.

Love what you are and love what others are in you.

SHARE IN A FEW LINES:

A SITUATION IN WHICH YOU LOVED A LOT AND RECEIVED LOVE.

....

....

....

SOMEONE WHO BROUGHT HEALING INTO YOUR LIFE.

....

....

....

A CHILDHOOD EPISODE THAT STILL INFLUENCES YOUR CHOICES.

....

....

....

A PAIN OR LOSS AND HOW YOU LEARNED TO LIVE WITH IT.

....

....

....

✦ SWORDS ✦

The Swords are associated with air; winter; intellect and mental strength; observation of the world around; and the unseen and its challenges, which can only be embraced and met with deep inner clarity. The mind is the seat of imagination, memory, and the ability to analyze, but in these things reside solutions such as deception, paranoia, and false beliefs about oneself.

It is therefore necessary to use the advice of the Swords with equal caution and decision.

GUIDING WORDS

ANALYSIS

MIND

PERCEPTION

IMAGINATION

COMMUNICATION

CLARITY

DECISION

UNCERTAINTY

MEDITATION

CONTROL

REMEMBER:

The sword divides shadow from light, but both are reflected in its blade.

The cut of the sword is irreparable.

Sometimes the sword is more effective if it remains in its scabbard.

Use the sword to discern what is right from what is not.

Do not point the sword at the helpless.

What the sword shatters can have new life elsewhere.

Every sword is also a mirror that reflects your soul. Free your heart and observe yourself.

SHARE IN A FEW LINES:

A SITUATION IN WHICH YOU HAD TO MAKE A DIFFICULT CHOICE.

....

....

....

A SITUATION IN WHICH YOU NEEDED HELP TO GET AWAY FROM SOMETHING THAT WAS OPPRESSING YOU.

....

....

....

A SITUATION IN WHICH RESOLVE AND DEEP TRUST IN YOUR VALUES GUIDED YOU.

....

....

....

A DECEPTIVE SITUATION THAT YOU SENSED, AND HOW YOU ACTED ON IT.

....

....

....

PENTACLES

The Pentacles are associated with the earth, the autumn harvest, material goods, family and traditions, goal achievement, work and talent, and the magical fulfillment of the work in which everything is held. Like the earth, the Pentacles suggest anticipation and an attention to detail that allows one to discern the plant from the seed. The materiality of Pentacles implies the ability to stably navigate in principles and affections.

GUIDING WORDS

MATERIALITY

CONCRETENESS

COOPERATION

PERSONAL RESOURCES

ENVIRONMENTAL RESOURCES

TALENT

ECOLOGY

MAGIC

BONDS

TRADITION

REMEMBER:

The Pentacle is a magic symbol.
Everything in it meets, reacts, and generates.

In the Pentacles is the value of spiritual work in harmony with material work.

You can rejoice in your work even before you see results.

In the Pentacles, you establish lasting bonds and connections with others.

The earth shelters us, feeds us, cares for us, lifts our spirits in pain. Let us travel on her temporarily. Let us respect her.

A Pentacle is a solid pledge. It asks you to learn to discern who to make covenants with.

In Pentacles you can decide what to keep and what to let go from your experience.

Share in a Few Lines:

A work experience that shaped and formed you.

....

....

....

A situation in which your value was widely recognized.

....

....

....

A long-standing friendship or relationship.

....

....

....

A situation in which you feel that forgetting is more valuable than keeping.

....

....

....

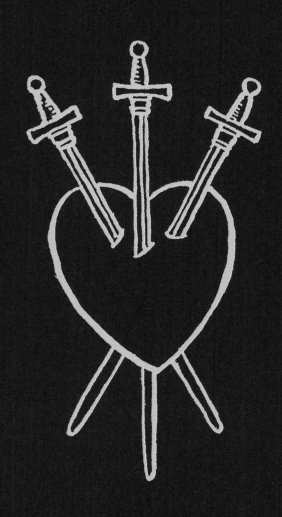

CHAPTER 3

MINOR ARCANA

✦ THE ACES ✦

 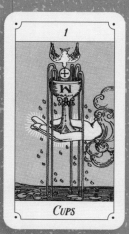  

WANDS CUPS SWORDS PENTACLES

"I am large, I contain multitudes."
WALT WHITMAN

The **Aces** embody the intelligence of each suit and its potential, which is ready to be unleashed. They represent the unity that reverberates in the multitudes and in self-control and control over one's actions. Each Ace is a principle associated with an action that shapes life through these **FOUR POWERS**:

+ **CREATION** in the Ace of Wands
+ **ACCEPTANCE** in the Ace of Cups
+ **JUSTICE** in the Ace of Swords
+ **FULFILLMENT** in the Ace of Pentacles

THESE FOUR POWERS
LEAD TO:

- **Wands:** contagious enthusiasm that upsets common sense
- **Cups:** the beauty of loving
- **Swords:** a determined and calm mind
- **Pentacles:** the joy of what grows everywhere

MESSAGES

- **Ace of Wands** - In good weather and bad, it continues to flourish.

- **Ace of Cups** - This is the cup of the heart; recognize its intelligence.

- **Ace of Swords** - Raise the sword and make light.

- **Ace of Pentacles** - Honor your roots and create new ones.

Share a Personal Episode When:

1. YOUR VALUE WAS RECOGNIZED AND APPRECIATED BY A LARGER OR SMALLER COMMUNITY.

....

....

....

....

....

2. YOU WELCOMED ANOTHER WITHOUT FEAR.

....

....

....

....

....

3. YOU MADE A CHOICE BY FOLLOWING INNER MORALITY.

....

....

....

....

....

....

....

4. YOU CELEBRATED YOUR ACHIEVEMENTS.

....

....

....

....

....

....

....

✦ The Twos ✦

WANDS

CUPS

SWORDS

PENTACLES

"It may be that a thing repulses you while it is good for you, and it may be that you love a thing while it is bad for you. God knows and you do not know."

QURAN, II, 201 6

The **Twos** indicate the choices on our path. In their presence we must stop, for the journey begins in the mind, where we weigh the possibilities, relying on what we know and intuition to take the first step through these **FOUR POWERS**:

- ✦ **ASSESSMENT** of potential in the Two of Wands
- ✦ **MEETING** and **FALLING IN LOVE** in the Two of Cups
- ✦ **SEARCH** for inner truth in the Two of Swords
- ✦ **MAINTENANCE** of vital balance in the Two of Pentacles

THESE FOUR POWERS
LEAD TO:

- ✦ **Wands:** a commitment to the future that is rooted in the present world
- ✦ **Cups:** denuding oneself before the other
- ✦ **Swords:** the ability to make choices when every goal is uncertain
- ✦ **Pentacles:** the ability to handle multiple things at once

MESSAGES

- ✦ **Two of Wands** - Observe the world in your hands and the world in front of you. Try to bring them together.

- ✦ **Two of Cups** - Proceed with kindness toward the other and see with their eyes.

- ✦ **Two of Swords** - Find a quiet place to meditate. Observe the landscape with your mind's eye.

- ✦ **Two of Pentacles** - In the game of infinity, each thing flows into the other.

SHARE A PERSONAL EPISODE WHEN:

1. YOU ABANDONED THE CERTAINTY OF WHAT YOU HAD FOR A BROADER HORIZON.

....

....

....

....

....

2. YOU EXPERIENCED KNOWLEDGE THROUGH LOVE.

....

....

....

....

....

3. YOU EXPERIENCED SOME THERAPY, RELYING ON OTHERS TO UNDERSTAND YOUR LIFE.

....

....

....

....

....

....

....

4. YOU PURSUED SEVERAL THINGS AT THE SAME TIME WITHOUT BECOMING EXHAUSTED.

....

....

....

....

....

....

THE THREES

WANDS

CUPS

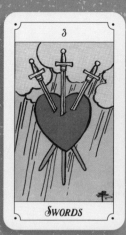
SWORDS

PENTACLES

"With strength from the south the sun, companion of the moon, / stretched out its right hand toward the edge of the sky; / the sun did not know where its home was; / the stars did not know they had a home; / the moon did not know what its power was."
VÖLUSPÁ

The four **Threes** represent creation, the growth that results from the union of two forces to generate another. In the Three, the vision is established and the work begins. We can recognize the first turning point through these **FOUR POWERS**:

- forward-looking **COMMITMENT** in the Three of Wands
- amicable **CONNECTION** in the Three of Cups
- living the **INTENSITY** of pain in the Three of Swords
- **COLLABORATION** in the Three of Pentacles

THESE FOUR POWERS LEAD TO:

- **Wands:** a life-redesigning project
- **Cups:** the shining of sisterhood
- **Swords:** the ability to learn from wounds
- **Pentacles:** the emergence of talent in the collective

MESSAGES

- **Three of Wands** - Watch the horizon when the sea is calm and recognize who shows up.

- **Three of Cups** - Celebrate your ancestors in the friendships of the present.

- **Three of Swords** - Expose your wounds without playing the victim.

- **Three of Pentacles** - True talent is not afraid of confrontation.

Share a personal episode when:

1. YOU WERE ABLE TO LOOK FORWARD WITH CONFIDENCE AND PAVE THE WAY FOR YOUR DREAMS.

....

....

....

....

2. YOU EXPERIENCED A SENSE OF EQUALITY, HAPPINESS, AND MUTUAL UNDERSTANDING IN FAMILY OR FRIENDSHIPS.

....

....

....

....

....

3. YOU HAVE MENDED A BROKEN HEART.

....

....

....

....

....

....

....

4. YOU HAVE WORKED WITH OTHERS TOWARD THE SUCCESS OF SOMETHING.

....

....

....

....

....

....

✦ The Fours ✦

WANDS

CUPS

SWORDS

PENTACLES

"Inhabit the house and it will not collapse."
ARSENY TARKOVSKY

In the **Fours**, we find stability, structure, and home. The four cardinal points, the four winds, the four walls that contain dreams. Here we can pause, find a definition of ourselves through these **FOUR POWERS**:

- ✦ **CELEBRATION** in the Four of Wands
- ✦ **CONTEMPLATION** in the Four of Cups
- ✦ **RECOVERY OF STRENGTH** in the Four of Swords
- ✦ **COMFORT OF ONE'S POSSESSIONS** in the Four of Pentacles

THESE FOUR POWERS
LEAD TO:

- ✦ **Wands:** a celebration before an important departure
- ✦ **Cups:** dissatisfaction or boredom that triggers movement
- ✦ **Swords:** restful sleep for a new dream
- ✦ **Pentacles:** the knowledge of one's limits and overcoming them

MESSAGES

- ✦ **Four of Wands** - Celebration is a temporary zone of joy where you can enjoy the embrace of the world.

- ✦ **Four of Cups** - The line between boredom and contemplation is thin; you only need to push the mind beyond appearances.

- ✦ **Four of Swords** - Life is also about sleep, rest, and healing.

- ✦ **Four of Pentacles** - It is useful to have a place where all our precious possessions, memories, gifts remain as long as you can detach from them when needed.

Share a Personal Episode When:

1. YOU REACHED A MILESTONE AND CELEBRATED WITH THOSE DEAR TO YOU.

....

....

....

....

....

2. YOU EXPERIENCED DISSATISFACTION AND BEGAN TO WANDER ELSEWHERE WITH YOUR THOUGHTS.

....

....

....

....

....

3. YOU EXPERIENCED ILLNESS, A HOSPITAL STAY, OR SIMILAR.

....

....

....

....

....

....

....

....

4. YOU BUILT YOUR PERSONAL SPACE.

....

....

....

....

....

....

....

◆ THE FIVES ◆

WANDS   CUPS   SWORDS   PENTACLES

"Trust the trail of tears
And learn to live."
PAUL CELAN

The **Fives** show crisis, rupture, and the decisive and formative difficulties one might encounter on their path. In the number Five, one can recognize the conflict and trial that are revealed through these **FOUR POWERS**:

- **TENSION** in the Five of Wands
- **LOSS OF AFFECTION** in the Five of Cups
- **DEFEAT** and **SURPRISE** in the Five of Swords
- **MATERIAL MISERY** in the Five of Pentacles

THESE FOUR POWERS
LEAD TO:

- **Wands:** the need to find a shared course, or else get lost in the chaos of personalities
- **Cups:** the possibility of healing by appreciating more of what remains whole
- **Swords:** understanding the offended within and giving them a voice
- **Pentacles:** recognizing shelters, outstretched hands, inner resources

MESSAGES

- **Five of Wands** - One must learn to resolve quarrels and petty conflicts for a common good.

- **Five of Cups** - Take time for suffering, but honor those who leave with love.

- **Five of Swords** - Recognize yourself in the oppressed, even when you are the victor.

- **Five of Pentacles** - Don't wander far from help; start asking and knocking on doors.

SHARE A PERSONAL EPISODE WHEN:

1. YOU ARGUED WITH OTHERS WITHOUT REACHING AN AGREEMENT OR LOSING SIGHT OF THE GOAL.

....

....

....

....

....

....

2. THE LOSS OF A LOVED ONE ABSORBED YOU ENTIRELY.

....

....

....

....

....

3. YOU SUFFERED AN INJUSTICE OR YOU HAVE COMMITTED ONE.

....
....
....
....
....
....
....
....

4. YOU ASKED FOR HELP AMID GREAT DIFFICULTY.

....
....
....
....
....
....
....

✦ The Sixes ✦

WANDS   CUPS   SWORDS   PENTACLES

*"Beauty is truth, truth beauty—that is all
ye know on earth, and all ye need only know."*
JOHN KEATS

The four **Sixes** can be read as a respite, a blessing that love brings into our lives. In the number Six, the harmony, grace, and beauty of all that exists are restored through these **FOUR POWERS**:

- **RECOGNITION** in the Six of Wands
- **REMEMBRANCE** in the Six of Cups
- **CROSSING** in the Six of Swords
- **GIFTS** in the Six of Pentacles

THESE FOUR POWERS
LEAD TO:

- + **Wands:** a shared victory and a homecoming
- + **Cups:** a sense of family belonging that transcends the law of time
- + **Swords:** a journey to an unknown shore where we can rely on others
- + **Pentacles:** an equitable exchange between giver and receiver, extending each other's hands

MESSAGES

- + **Six of Wands** - To return means to be recognized by another and to find a home in them.

- + **Six of Swords** - Much of life is not a landing but a crossing, in which others show the path.

- + **Six of Cups** - In the world of memory, time gains its meaning, overcoming life and death in love.

- + **Six of Pentacles** - There is no humiliation in reaching out a hand to ask, no waste in giving to those who ask with clarity.

Share a Personal Episode When:

1. YOUR VALUE WAS RECOGNIZED AND APPRECIATED BY A LARGER OR SMALLER COMMUNITY.

....

....

....

....

....

2. YOU FOUND REFUGE IN A HAPPY MEMORY WHERE THOSE YOU LOVE ARE PRESENT.

....

....

....

....

....

3. YOU EMBARKED ON AN IMPORTANT TRANSFORMATIVE JOURNEY AND WERE HELPED BY SOMEONE.

....

....

....

....

....

....

....

4. YOU GAVE OR RECEIVED, KNOWING WHEN AND FROM WHOM TO ASK OR GIVE.

....

....

....

....

....

....

◆ THE SEVENS ◆

WANDS

CUPS

SWORDS

PENTACLES

"Truth is a matter of imagination."
URSULA K. LE GUIN

The four **Sevens** present the reversal of harmony, along with individual resources that may be hidden even from ourselves. Seven is a magic number whose inspiration is manifested through these **FOUR POWERS**:

- **PERSONAL DEFENSE** in the Seven of Wands
- **SPIRITUAL SEARCH** in the Seven of Cups
- **NONCONFORMITY** in the Seven of Swords
- **WAITING** in the Seven of Pentacles

THESE FOUR POWERS
LEAD TO:

- ╀ **Wands:** a resolute affirmation of self
- ╀ **Cups:** enter reality once illusions are recognized
- ╀ **Swords:** hide the secret weapon, surprising and getting away with one's truth
- ╀ **Pentacles:** rejoice in the work done and enjoy its fruits without haste

MESSAGES

- ╀ **Seven of Wands** - Remember that a free and honest mind is the best armor.

- ╀ **Seven of Cups** - Time is not only about goals, but also about moments to wander in imagination.

- ╀ **Seven of Swords** - Find your way, subvert order, survive.

- ╀ **Seven of Pentacles** - Fulfillment in existing is often the long moment when you understand that everything is about to blossom.

Share a Personal Episode When:

1. YOU HAD TO DEFEND WHAT YOU LOVE AND BELIEVE IN SUCCESSFULLY.

....

....

....

....

....

2. YOU GOT LOST IN DAYDREAMS, AND IT WAS VERY BEAUTIFUL.

....

....

....

....

....

3. YOU TOLD A LIE OR PLAYED SMART BY CATCHING EVERYONE BY SURPRISE.

....

....

....

....

....

....

....

4. YOU ENJOYED BOTH THE WAIT AND THE REAPING.

....

....

....

....

....

....

THE EIGHTS

WANDS

CUPS

SWORDS

PENTACLES

"The force that through the green fuse drives the flower."
DYLAN THOMAS

Commitment and the pursuit of purpose in reality shine in the **Eights**. The Eight can turn into the symbol for infinity, just as devotion to work provides for its success and continuous renewal through these **FOUR POWERS**:

- **READINESS** in the Eight of Wands
- **COURAGE** in the Eight of Cups
- **ENDURANCE** in the Eight of Swords
- **PRACTICALITY** in the Eight of Pentacles

THESE FOUR POWERS
LEAD TO:

+ **Wands:** seize the opportunity when it presents itself
+ **Cups:** know how to move away from certainty to follow one's path
+ **Swords:** free oneself from doubts, terrors, and even the violence suffered
+ **Pentacles:** realize something unique and beautiful

MESSAGES

+ **Eight of Wands** - Seize the moment; recognize the message.

+ **Eight of Cups** - Prepare for life's journey: the mountain is high, but the home is within you.

+ **Eight of Swords** - The worst traps are the ones we create for ourselves.

+ **Eight of Pentacles** - It is a rare blessing to be able to devote ourselves to what we love. When it happens, do it with your whole self.

Share a Personal Episode When:

1. YOU RECEIVED UNEXPECTED NEWS AND ACTED POSITIVELY AS A RESULT.

....

....

....

....

....

2. YOU LEFT YOUR COMFORT ZONE TO VENTURE INTO THE MYSTERIES OF THE WORLD BY FOLLOWING DREAMS.

....

....

....

....

....

3. YOU EXPERIENCED A SENSE OF ENTRAPMENT, FEAR, AND DENIAL AND YET DID NOT GIVE IN.

....

....

....

....

....

....

....

4. YOU COMPLETED SOMETHING BY ADDRESSING IT DOWN TO THE SMALLEST DETAIL.

....

....

....

....

....

....

....

THE NINES

WANDS

CUPS

SWORDS

PENTACLES

"The fear of growing old comes at the moment when one recognizes that one is not living the life one desires. It is equivalent to the feeling of abusing the present."
SUSAN SONTAG

In the four **Nines**, the journey is almost complete. We know the substance of our being and the most authentic challenge of existence; we embrace the universal value of living. Everything is ready and we can be the center of it through these **FOUR POWERS**:

- **RESILIENCE** in the Nine of Wands
- **GENEROSITY** in the Nine of Cups
- **UNCERTAINTY** of despair in the Nine of Swords
- **WEALTH** in the Nine of Pentacles

THESE FOUR POWERS LEAD TO:

- **Wands:** the ability to withstand bumps and pull out charisma in extreme moments
- **Cups:** the clear willingness to embrace and share what we have
- **Swords:** emancipating ourselves from the consequences of trauma, treasuring it
- **Pentacles:** learning the benefits of creative solitude

MESSAGES

- **Nine of Wands** - Don't give in, regain your strength by focusing on beauty.

- **Nine of Swords** - Whenever trauma repeats itself, in life or in the mind, trust in recovery.

- **Nine of Cups** - Open all doors. Nothing is lost; everything comes back.

- **Nine of Pentacles** - Protect a world of your own in the world of others.

SHARE A PERSONAL EPISODE WHEN:

1. YOU EXPERIENCED WEARINESS BUT DID NOT SURRENDER.

....

....

....

....

....

2. YOU ENRICHED YOUR SOUL THROUGH THE PRESENCE OF OTHERS.

....

....

....

....

....

3. YOU HAVE EXPERIENCED A TRAUMATIC PERIOD.

....

....

....

....

....

....

....

....

4. YOU DID EXACTLY EVERYTHING YOU WANTED TO DO.

....

....

....

....

....

....

....

✦ THE TENS ✦

| 10 | 10 | 10 | 10 |
| WANDS | CUPS | SWORDS | PENTACLES |

*"Night arrives
in a column of love and nightingales"*
EUNICE HATE

In the **Tens**, we find the final push, the completed goal, the closing of a phase, or the highest expression of a feeling. In Number Ten, one cycle concludes and another is inaugurated through these **FOUR POWERS**:

+ **FATIGUE** in the Ten of Wands
+ **JOY** in the Ten of Cups
+ **ENDING** in the Ten of Swords
+ **FAMILY** in the Ten of Pentacles

THESE FOUR POWERS
LEAD TO:

- **Wands:** the need to get rid of excessive burdens
- **Cups:** knowing how to make memories from every bit of beauty
- **Swords:** not indulging in something that cannot be revived
- **Pentacles:** expanding one's emotional boundaries

MESSAGES

- **Ten of Wands** - What happens is not solely your responsibility. Recognize your duties and those of others.

- **Ten of Cups** - A rainbow is a promise of reconciliation and lightness of heart.

- **Ten of Swords** - Do not persist where any feeling or possibility has stopped growing.

- **Ten of Pentacles** - A happy home is one where many are welcome.

SHARE A PERSONAL EPISODE WHEN:

1. YOU CARRIED BURDENS THAT WERE NOT YOURS TO BEAR.

....

....

....

....

....

2. YOU HAVE KNOWN THE MOST INTENSE HAPPINESS WITH SOMEONE.

....

....

....

....

....

3. YOU REALIZED THAT YOU HAD TO GET OUT OF A DEAD-END SITUATION.

....

....

....

....

....

....

....

4. YOU CARED FOR ALL THE MEMBERS OF YOUR FAMILY.

....

....

....

....

....

....

....

CHAPTER 4

COURT
CARDS

The Court cards are **THE PEOPLE OF THE DECK**, in which we might **RECOGNIZE SOMEONE REAL**, a person in one's family or friend circle, a famous person, an aspect of ourselves. The best way to explore them is to draw on one's daily experience.

Before we delve into the figures and their meanings, let's play **A GAME**.

Lay out all the Court cards in front of you and observe them. Intuitively choose a few by answering these questions with a brief description:

◆ **WHICH OF THE COURT CARDS HAVE YOU BEEN?**

....
....
....

◆ **WHO ARE YOU NOW?**

....
....
....

◆ **WHO WOULD YOU LIKE TO HAVE BEEN?**

....
....
....

◆ **HOW DO YOU SEE THE FUTURE DEVELOPMENT OF YOUR PERSON?**

....

....

....

....

◆ **WHICH PERSON IN THE COURT INSPIRES CONFIDENCE IN YOU?**

....

....

....

....

◆ **AND WHICH REPULSION?**

....

....

....

....

◆ **WHO AMONG THE COURT CARDS WOULD YOU WANT AS YOUR CHOSEN ADVENTURE COMPANION?**

....

....

....

....

◆ THE PAGE ◆

PAGE OF WANDS

PAGE OF CUPS

PAGE OF SWORDS

PAGE OF PENTACLES

> *"I'm youth, I'm joy,*
> *I'm a little bird that has broken out of the egg."*
> JAMES MATTHEW BARRIE

The four **Pages** represent learning, experience, childhood as a curious approach to the world. The Pages embody the spirit of youth, which can rise again at any age. This spirit **MANIFESTS**:

-+- as **ENTHUSIASM** in the Page of Wands
-+- as **SENSITIVITY** in the Page of Cups
-+- as **WIT** in the Page of Swords
-+- as **STUDY** in the Page of Pentacles

LOOK AT THE FOUR PAGES AND RESPOND INTUITIVELY:

Do you recognize anyone familiar? Give a brief description of the people you identify in one or more of them.

....

....

....

....

NOW DESCRIBE EACH PAGE, FOLLOWING THESE SUGGESTIONS:

PAGE OF WANDS:

A game I loved in childhood.
Something I invented.

....

....

....

....

PAGE OF CUPS:

A romantic dream I carry with me.
In whom and what I place my trust.

....

....

....

....

PAGE OF SWORDS:

An important message you had to deliver.
When you had to mediate between parties.

....

....

....

....

....

....

PAGE OF PENTACLES:

An experience of study and research.
A change you went through to begin work.

....

....

....

....

....

....

....

✦ Knights ✦

Knight of Wands

Knight of Cups

Knight of Swords

Knight of Pentacles

> *"What is not accomplished drives*
> *the way of proceeding,*
> *Goal, goal, burn and reburn,*
> *during the coast of the millennia."*
> ### Patrizia Vicinelli

The four **Knights** personify action, constant forward movement, stepping into life with purpose. The age of choices, rebellion, and independence **MANIFESTS** itself in the spirit of the Knights in these ways:

+ with **CHARISMA** in the Knight of Wands
+ with **ROMANTIC PURSUIT** in the Knight of Cups
+ with **DETERMINATION** in the Knight of Swords
+ with **SLOWNESS** in the Knight of Pentacles

LOOK AT THE FOUR KNIGHTS AND RESPOND INTUITIVELY:

Do you recognize anyone familiar? Give a brief description of the people you identify in one or more of them.

....

....

....

....

Now describe each Knight, following these suggestions:

KNIGHT OF WANDS:

A situation in which you acted as a leader or guide.
Something or someone that awakens your desire to do things.

....

....

....

....

KNIGHT OF CUPS:

An important romance.
A time when you did not show your feelings.

....

....

....

....

....

KNIGHT OF SWORDS:
Something you threw yourself into entirely.
A fixed idea that animated your choices.

....

....

....

....

....

....

KNIGHT OF PENTACLES:
The things you discovered as you slowly moved forward.
Concern for animals and nature.

....

....

....

....

....

....

....

✦ Queens ✦

QUEEN OF WANDS

QUEEN OF CUPS

QUEEN OF SWORDS

QUEEN OF PENTACLES

> *"In my time I have been called many things: sister, lover, priestess, wise-woman, queen. Now in truth I have come to be wise-woman, and a time may come when these things may need to be known."*
> ### MARION ZIMMER BRADLEY

In the four **Queens**, we are confronted with the creative force of the element they embody, which leads to openness toward others. The artistic and conscious expression of the suit **IS MANIFESTED** in the spirit of the Queens in these ways:

- with **PASSION** in the Queen of Wands
- with **COMPASSION** in the Queen of Cups
- with **AUTONOMY** in the Queen of Swords
- with **GIVING** in the Queen of Pentacles

LOOK AT THE FOUR QUEENS AND RESPOND INTUITIVELY:

Do you recognize anyone familiar? Give a brief description of the people you identify in one or more of them.

....

....

....

....

Now describe each Queen, following these suggestions:

QUEEN OF WANDS:
Describe the witch who inhabits you.
Think of an unusual, offbeat, creative figure who inspired you.

....

....

....

....

QUEEN OF CUPS:
A woman (or man) in your life who brings healing.
What do you see in the cup of your heart?

....

....

....

....

QUEEN OF SWORDS:

A moment when you claimed your full autonomy.
A difficult decision you made for the benefit of yourself and others.

....

....

....

....

....

....

QUEEN OF PENTACLES:

A celebration for which you were the center, creator, and soul.
A list of what you know how to give.

....

....

....

....

....

....

✦ Kings ✦

King of Wands

Kings of Cups

King of Swords

King of Pentacles

"You are a man, little brother,
wolfling of my watching."
RUDYARD KIPLING

In **Kings**, we find the authority of power, experience, taking of command, and good counsel. The spirit of Kings is the true keeper of the energy of the suit, which **IS EXPRESSED** in these ways:

- + with **LEADERSHIP** in the King of Wands
- + with **BENEVOLENCE** in the King of Cups
- + with **OVERALL VISION** in the King of Swords
- + with **ABUNDANCE** in the King of Pentacles.

LOOK AT THE FOUR KINGS AND RESPOND INTUITIVELY:

Do you recognize anyone familiar? Give a brief description of the people you identify in one or more of them.

....

....

....

....

NOW DESCRIBE EACH KING, FOLLOWING THESE SUGGESTIONS:

KING OF WANDS:
Describe a charismatic and authoritative person.
When you inspired others or were inspired.

....

....

....

....

....

KING OF CUPS:
Someone you asked for personal relationship advice.
When you were able to look at your emotional life with detachment
and clarity.

....

....

....

....

KING OF SWORDS:
A situation whose outcome you were able to foresee.
A seemingly cold but wise and honest person.

....

....

....

....

....

....

KING OF PENTACLES:
A generous, cheerful figure in your life.
A hospitable place where you have enjoyed the company of others.

....

....

....

....

....

....

CHAPTER 5

SPREADS AND EXERCISES

MIRROR SPREAD

To understand more about the **Major Arcana,** you can try this spread. Divide the deck into five groups: **Major Arcana**, **Wands**, **Cups, Swords,** and **Pentacles.** Draw a **Major Arcana** card and then a card from each suit to place under it.

The spread will tell you how the Arcana card is currently reflected and acting in the various areas of your life.

+ **Wands:** work, creativity, projects

+ **Cups:** feelings, internal life, relationships

+ **Swords:** intellect, communication, study

+ **Pentacles:** material goods, family, business

0

THE FOOL

6	2	10	5
WANDS	CUPS	PENTACLES	SWORDS

LIGHT

A fragment of a star lives in each of us, **guiding** and **comforting us in life**. It grows with us; sometimes its light is dim and dying, other times it blazes, but it never fails. With tarot cards, we can recognize it by looking for **our guiding cards**, which can vary depending on the moment.

Look at the 78 cards in the deck and instinctively **draw a maximum of five** that strike you as **beautiful** and **familiar**.

+ What do you see in them?

+ Describe the scene as it appears before your eyes.

+ Describe how you feel.

+ Describe a moment in your life that you recognize in the image.

JUDGMENT

CUPS

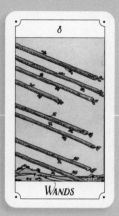

WANDS

SWORDS

THE EMPRESS

Shadow

What is a Shadow? **The dark and hidden aspect of our lives, the fears of the soul,** its **fragilities.** Yet the Shadow is **also a point of strength, a place of solace** where we can take refuge and begin again. It is possible to work on this intuitively with tarot cards, through some simple exercises.

1. LOOKING AT THE SHADOW

Look at the 78 cards in the deck and instinctively **draw a maximum of five** that make you **feel uncomfortable** but which **nonetheless speak powerfully** to you.

+ What do you see in them?
+ Describe the scene as it appears before your eyes.
+ Describe how you feel.
+ Describe a moment in your life that you recognize in the image.

KINGS OF CUPS

XIII

DEATH

VIII

STRENGTH

1

SWORDS

3

WANDS

2. PASSING THROUGH THE SHADOW

You can proceed with an easy spread by shuffling the deck and **drawing seven cards,** placing them in the **shape of an arrow** as shown in the picture.

1. Situation

2. What are the hidden feelings?

3. What must I not forget?

4. What do I need to let go of?

5. How is the Shadow reflected in my state of mind and behavior?

6. How does the Shadow affect my relationship with others?

7. Where can I find help and advice?

4

3

SWORDS

5

IV

LOVERS

1

QUEEN OF SWORDS

2

1

WANDS

7

PAGE OF CUPS

6

7

CUPS

3

8

PENTACLES

Spread for the Home

Your home is a space of refuge, comfort, and preparation. How do you live it? With this quick spread, you can recreate a space for personal meditation.

Draw four cards and arrange them in a square, proceeding clockwise from top left to bottom left.

Leave a blank space in the center.

1. The entrance: who and what you let in.

2. The kitchen: what you are creating for your life.

3. The studio: the advice you need.

4. The bedroom: your dreams for the future.

Now draw the fifth card that represents you inside the house and arrange it in the center. Do you recognize yourself?

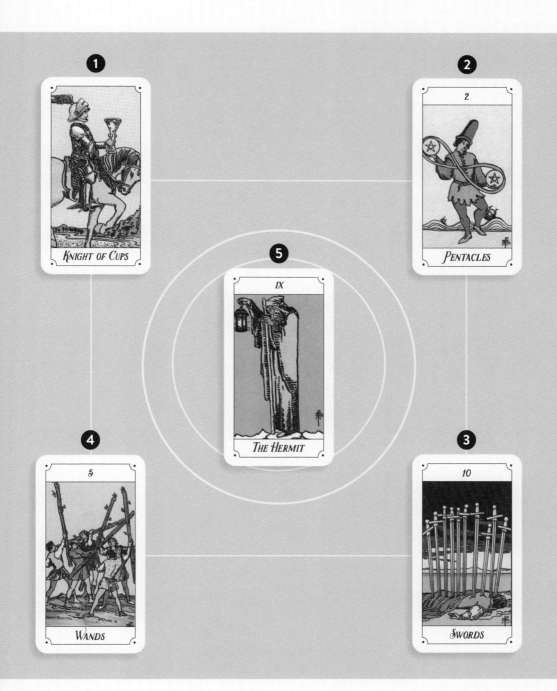

1 — KNIGHT OF CUPS

2 — 2 PENTACLES

5 — IX THE HERMIT

4 — 5 WANDS

3 — 10 SWORDS

CREATE A FAIRY TALE WITH TAROT CARDS

Shuffle the deck. **Draw a minimum of six to a maximum of ten cards** and reveal them in front of you.

Now **put them in a sequence that creates a story** that makes sense and includes them all. Some of them will represent characters, others situations.

Write down what you see and imagine.
You can repeat this exercise as many times as you like.

....

....

....

....

....

DRAW A MINIMUM OF SIX TO A MAXIMUM OF TEN CARDS.

KING OF CUPS

DEATH

STRENGTH

SWORDS

WANDS

PENTACLES

NOW PUT THEM IN A SEQUENCE THAT CREATES A STORY.

PENTACLES

STRENGTH

DEATH

KINGS OF CUPS

SWORDS

WANDS

WRITE A POEM WITH TAROT CARDS

In this book, there were many inspirational phrases and verses, which sometimes helped you understand the card and sometimes subverted the more classical approach. Now **try writing a poem yourself using the cards**.

You can play this game **either with cards face up**, consciously choosing them, **or with cards face down**, trusting in fate.

Draw six cards and **arrange them in a sequence** that is meaningful to you.

Write a couplet (two verses) for each card. In the first, focus on what you see. In the second, look at how this card interacts with you.

You can write as many poems as you like. The possibilities are endless.

DRAW SIX CARDS, FACE DOWN OR FACE UP.

| SWORDS | THE SUN | PENTACLES | WANDS | CUPS | QUEEN OF CUPS |

ARRANGE THEM IN A SEQUENCE THAT IS MEANINGFUL TO YOU.

| THE SUN | QUEEN OF CUPS | CUPS | WANDS | PENTACLES | SWORDS |

NOTES

NOTES

NOTES

NOTES

Francesca Matteoni

Francesca is a poet and writer. She has worked as a researcher, studying witchcraft, folklore, and medical beliefs and has published the academic article *Il famiglio della strega. Sangue e stregoneria nell'Inghilterra moderna* (Aras, 2014). She teaches history, anthropology, and literature at the American AIFS program in Florence. Some of her most recent publications include the book *Dal Matto al Mondo. Viaggio poetico nei tarocchi* (effequ, 2019); a piece on sacred plants in the book *La scommessa psichedelica* (Quodlibet, 2020) by Federico Di Vita; the book of poetry *Ciò che il mondo separa* (Marcos y Marcos, 2021) and the collection *Io sarò il rovo. Fiabe di un paese silenzioso* (effequ, 2021). She also writes books on magic, tarot cards, and oracles in collaboration with various illustrators, including themed tarot card decks *Ask the Witch Tarot, Grunge Tarot, Faeries and Magical Creatures,* and the book *Novice Witches and Apprentice Wizards: An Essential Handbook of Magic.*